P9-CBJ-024

A Bird's Body

JOANNA COLE
photographs by Jerome Wexler

William Morrow and Company
New York 1982

Drawing on page 9 from *Birds: Readings from Scientific American.* With introductions by Barry W. Wilson. Copyright © 1980 by Scientific American, Inc. All rights reserved.
All other drawings by Cynthia Basil.
Design by Cynthia Basil.

Library of Congress Cataloging in Publication Data

Cole, Joanna.
  A bird's body.
  Summary: Discusses the anatomy, characteristics, and behavior of birds, focusing on their ability to fly.
  1. Birds—Anatomy—Juvenile literature. 2. Birds—Physiology—Juvenile literature.
[1. Birds. 2. Flight] I. Wexler, Jerome, ill. II. Title.
QL697.C64   598.2'4   82-6446
ISBN 0-688-01470-4   AACR2
ISBN 0-688-01471-2 (lib. bdg.)

For his helpful reading of the manuscript, the author thanks George A. Clark, Jr., Ph.D., Associate Professor of Biology, The University of Connecticut.

Author's Note: The bird that is known as a parakeet in the United States is called a budgerigar, or budgie for short, in other parts of the world. Although "budgerigar" is the correct name, I have used "parakeet" in this book to avoid confusion among American readers.

If you see a flying animal that is not a bat or an insect, it must be a bird. No other animals have mastered the ability of true flight—except perhaps the prehistoric flying reptiles known as pterosaurs, and they are now extinct.

Of all the animals that can fly, birds are the champions. They can cruise easily at speeds of twenty to fifty miles an hour, and they can fly for a thousand miles or more without stopping. A bird's body almost seems to have been designed by nature as a living flying machine.

The pictures here are close-up views of two pet birds, a parakeet and a cockatiel, both members of the parrot family. Because you usually see these birds in cages, you may not think of them as expert fliers. But on the dry lands of Australia, where they live in the wild, they migrate in large flocks, often flying many miles to find food and water.

The ancestor of these and other birds was probably a prehistoric reptile that could not fly. Although birds seem very different from the snakes and lizards of today, scientists recognize that their skeleton, muscles, and brain have parts that are like those of reptiles. And, the scales on a bird's legs and feet are very much like a reptile's scales.

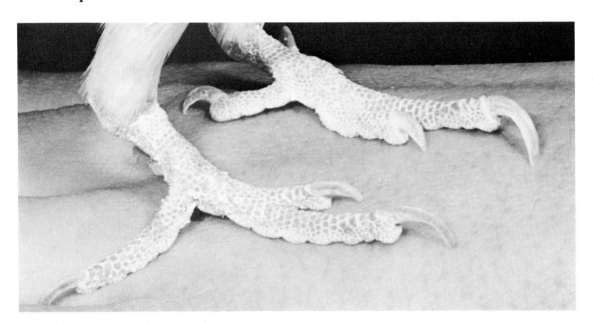

snake's skin

The prehistoric bird *Archaeopteryx* had feathers but still had many features of reptiles: teeth in the mouth, claws on the wings, and tailbones under the feathers.

In other ways, however, birds are different from today's reptiles. They are warm-blooded, and their heart is more like a mammal's heart than a reptile's. And one feature sets birds apart from *every* other animal: they are the only creatures in the world that have feathers.

Except for its beak, feet, and legs, a bird is completely covered with feathers. There are different kinds of feathers for different uses.

Smooth contour feathers cover a bird's body, wings, and tail. These feathers give the bird its streamlined contour, or shape. A contour feather has a stiff shaft in the center and a flat web, or vane, on each side.

contour feather

Beneath the contour feathers, many birds have a layer of fluffy down feathers for warmth.

Some birds have special ornamental feathers for decoration. The cockatiel, for instance, has crest feathers on its head.

down feather

ornamental feathers

11

Of all the feathers, the most important for flying are the contour feathers on the wing. They are known as the flight feathers.

The flight feathers are attached to the bird's wing bones. Because the bird's ancestors did not fly, the origin of the wing was a foreleg, or arm. The inner part of the wing is made up of the arm bones, while the outer tip is supported by the hand bones. Many of the hand and finger bones are fused together, but the thumb bone is still separate.

There are three kinds of flight feathers. The ones at the outer edge of the wing are attached to the hand bones. These long feathers are very important for flying and are called "primaries," or first feathers.

The ones that attach to the forearm bones are called "secondaries," or second feathers. And those that attach to the upper arm bone are called "tertiaries," or third feathers.

These feathers may look simple, but each one is actually a complicated structure. A single flight feather can have more than a million parts!

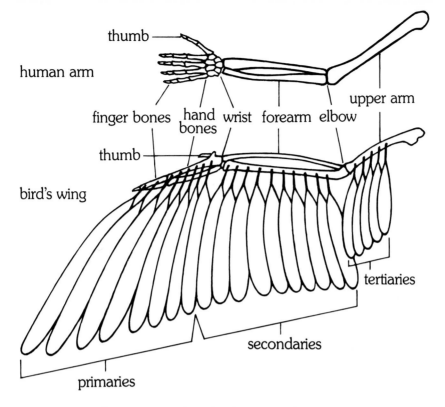

thumb

human arm

finger bones   hand   wrist   forearm   elbow

bones

upper arm

thumb

bird's wing

tertiaries

secondaries

primaries

13

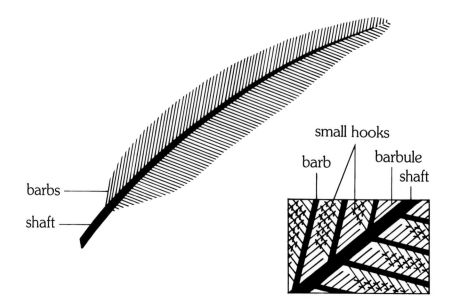

barbs

shaft

small hooks

barb

barbule

shaft

On each side of the feather's central shaft is a flat web, which is made up of hundreds of smaller shafts called "barbs." Branching out from each barb are hundreds of still smaller shafts called "barbules." And on each barbule are hundreds of tiny hooks that can be seen only through a microscope. These hooks hold the barbules together and keep the feather in shape.

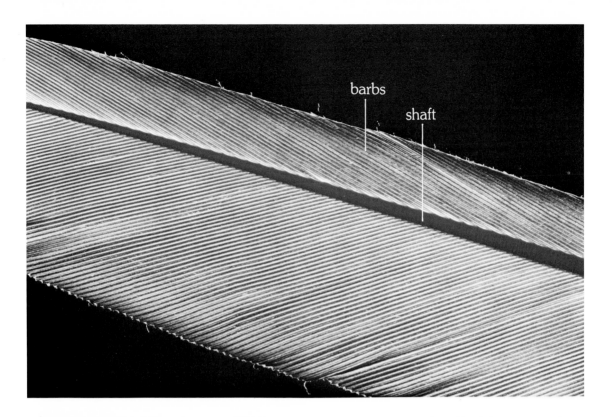

barbs

shaft

barbules

barb

15

As the bird moves around, the barbs may be pulled apart. When this happens, the bird "zips" them up again by drawing the feather through its beak. This is known as preening the feathers. A bird works hard to keep its feathers in good flying order. It may spend several hours each day preening.

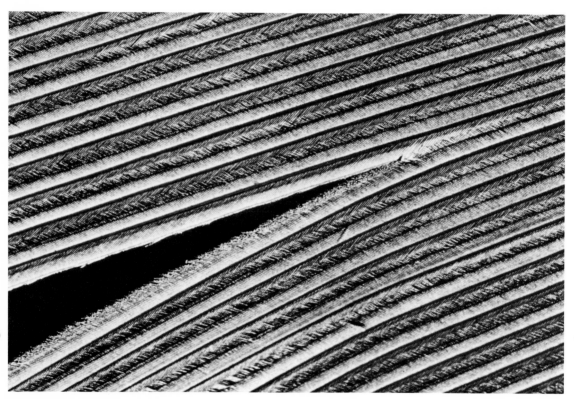

16

17

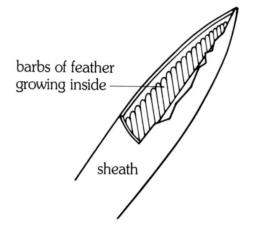

barbs of feather
growing inside

sheath

Once or twice a year birds molt,
or shed, the old feathers. When
feathers become worn, they are
pushed out a few at a time by new
ones.

A new feather grows inside a
horny sheath. When the new feather
is fully formed, the sheath splits
open. On the parakeet's head, you
can see the sheaths of some new
feathers.

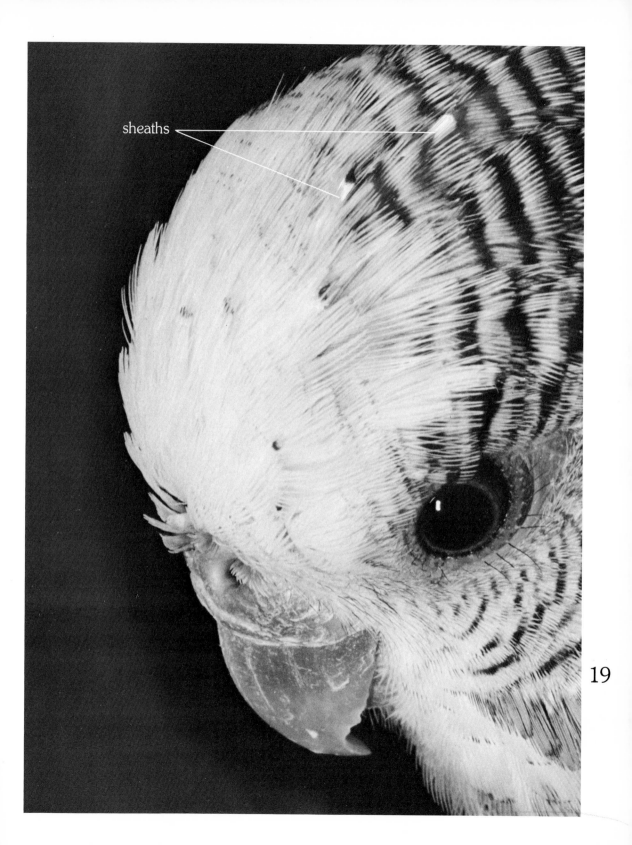

sheaths

19

The heavier a flying machine is, the more energy it uses to fly. To save energy, a flying machine is built to be as light as possible. A bird is also built for lightness.

Its bones are extra thin, and many of them are hollow. Its feathers have hollow shafts. Even a bird's mouth probably developed as a way of reducing weight. Instead of heavy jawbones and teeth, a bird has a lightweight beak made of thin horny material.

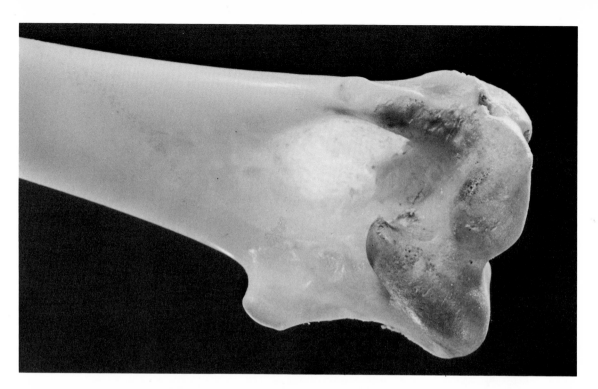

21

Once in the air, the lightweight, feathered bird is beautiful to see. People have always dreamed of winging through the air like birds. They have always wondered how birds could fly.

In the past, people thought that birds used their wings as oars and "rowed" through the air. But by studying slow-motion films, scientists have found out that birds do not fly this way at all. Amazingly, they fly almost the same way that propeller airplanes do.

23

The special shape of its wing is what keeps a plane up. This shape is called an "airfoil." The bottom of an airfoil is flat, but the top is curved. When air flows past the wing, it breaks up and meets again behind the wing. The air on top of the wing has to go faster to get over the curve. This fast-moving air on top pulls away from the wing. At the same time, the slow-moving air on the bottom pushes up on the wing.

The pulling on top and the pushing on the bottom are called "lift." Lift is what keeps a plane in the air.

To move forward, the plane uses propellers, which are like little spinning airfoils. In a sense, the propellers create lift that pulls forward instead of up.

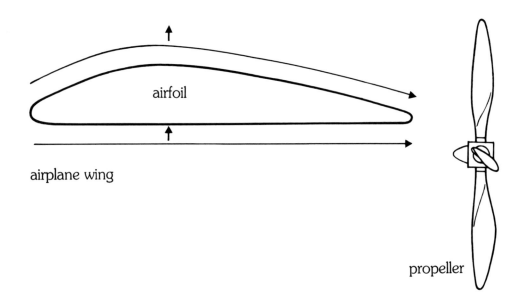

airfoil

airplane wing

propeller

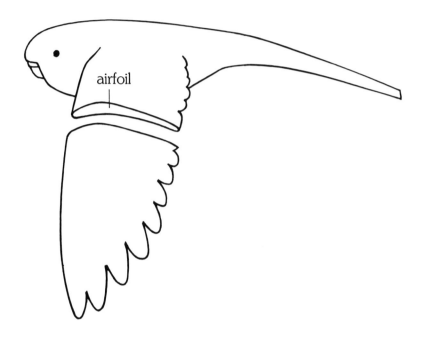

airfoil

How can a bird fly like a plane? Where are the airfoils and the propellers? One part of the bird's wing acts like an airfoil, and another part acts like a propeller.

The inner part of the wing, the arm, acts like an airfoil and provides lift. This inner wing is even shaped like a plane's wing.

25

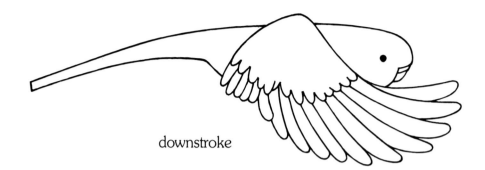

downstroke

The primary feathers on the outer part of the wing, the hand, act like propellers and move the bird forward. Of course, they don't spin around like a plane's propellers, but they do change position every time the bird flaps its wings.

On the downstroke, the wing moves down and forward until the primary feathers are even with the beak. At this point, for a tiny fraction of a second, the primary feathers twist around and face front. Air flows over them, and they act like little airfoils. They give the bird the same "forward-pulling lift" that the propeller gives the plane.

26

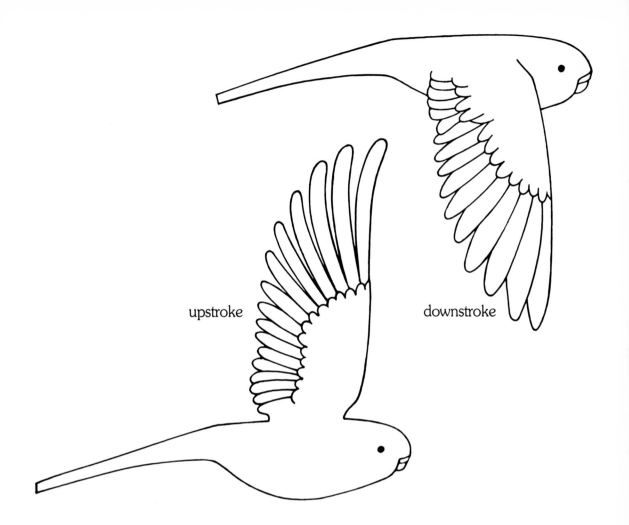

upstroke

downstroke

As the bird flies, all its flight feathers are constantly changing position. On the downstroke, the flight feathers close tightly together to form a solid mass. On the upstroke, they move apart to let air flow through them like the slats of a window blind.

For balance, the bird moves its tail feathers up, down, or to either side. For steering, it tips its wings from side to side.

27

On the ground, birds get around by walking, hopping, or climbing. Birds of the parrot family are good climbers.

Most birds have three of the four toes facing front. But many climbing birds have only two toes facing front, while the other two toes face back. The back toes serve as props, or braces.

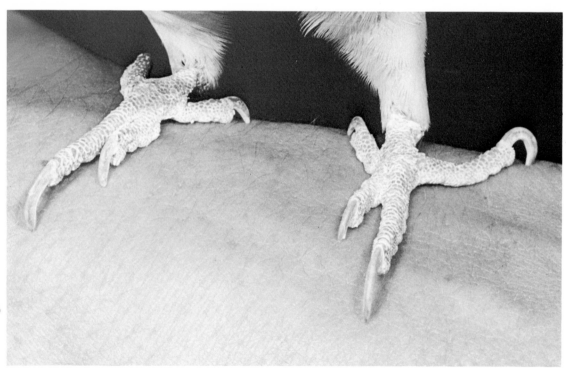

Parrots and their relatives also use the beak as a "third foot" when climbing.

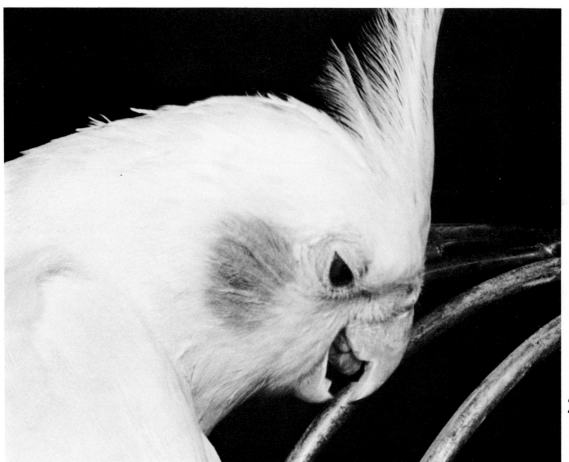

Flying requires a high level of energy. Birds get the extra energy they need by eating more food than other animals of the same size. Also, they eat only energy-rich foods, like seeds, fruits, fish, small rodents, worms, and insects. Birds almost never eat low-calorie foods like leaves or grass as their main diet.

Parakeets and cockatiels are seed-eaters. In nature, they live on ripe crops of wild grass seed.

31

An extra-efficient digestive system helps a bird get energy from its food as fast as possible. In some birds, food passes through the system in less than half an hour!

When food is eaten, it goes first to a large storage place called the "crop." The bird can swallow a lot of food quickly, store it in the crop, and then fly to a safe place to digest it.

From the crop, the food passes to the stomach. There digestive juices start to break the food down.

Then the food goes to the gizzard, a special grinding organ that takes the place of teeth. The gizzard's powerful muscles grind the food against hard ridges on the lining of the gizzard. To help the grinding, the bird swallows grit, or small stones, which also rub against the food. One experiment showed that a gizzard is so strong that a turkey could grind up steel needles!

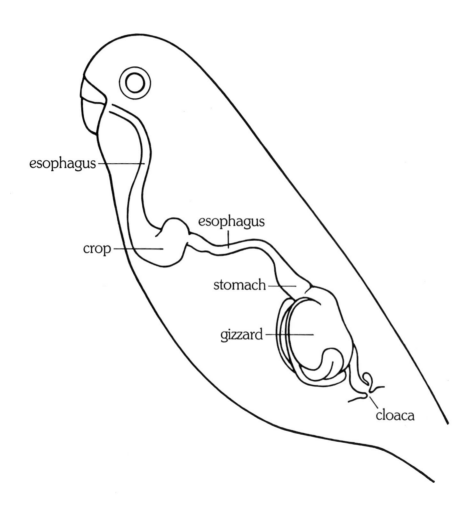

esophagus

esophagus

crop

stomach

gizzard

cloaca

33

To get extra energy, birds also use more oxygen than other animals of the same size. Although birds' lungs are rather small, they actually take in more oxygen than the larger lungs of other animals. The reason is that birds have a system of air sacs connected to the lungs.

Most animals have fresh air in their lungs only when they breathe in. But birds have fresh air in their lungs when they breathe in *and* when they breathe out. When a bird breathes in, part of the fresh air goes into the lungs and part is stored in the air sacs. Then when the bird breathes out, the stale air leaves the lungs and the unused air from the air sacs replaces it. In this way, there is a flow of fresh, oxygen-rich air passing through the lungs at all times.

The bird's heart pumps blood, which carries oxygen to all parts of the body. The heart of a bird is larger and beats faster than the hearts of other small animals. The heart of a small bird in flight may beat more than 500 times a minute. By comparison, a frog's heart beats only about 22 times a minute.

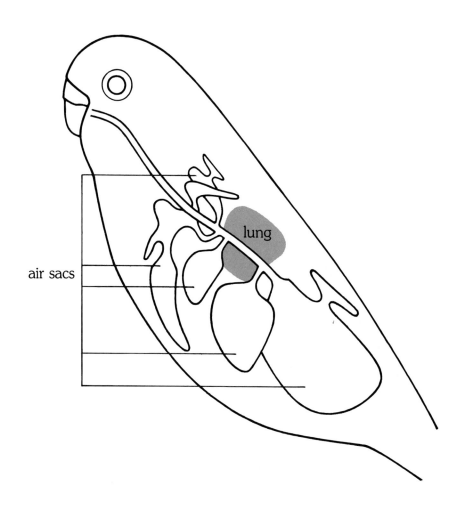

air sacs

lung

Like other animals, birds find out what is happening around them through their senses. For a bird, the most important sense is vision. Since they fly high, birds need good vision to see the earth below. Some birds can see eight times more sharply than human beings.

Although a bird's eyes are very large for its size, they do not look large because only a small part of the huge eyeball can be seen. The rest is hidden inside the eye socket. In most birds, the eyeballs are larger in bulk than the bird's entire brain.

The cockatiel's eyes are placed on the sides of its head, so it can see in almost a complete circle. When it looks at something in front, it cocks its head to one side. The bird seems to be wondering about something you just said, but actually it is fixing you with the area of sharpest vision in one eye.

37

Most birds use their sight rather than their sense of smell or taste to find and identify food. Their senses of smell and taste are usually very poor. While human beings have about 9000 taste buds on the tongue, a bird has less than 100.

The sense of touch is an important one for birds of the parrot family too. There are many touch nerves in the beak and in the cere, the patch of skin between the beak and the forehead. The cere has another function also. You can tell the sex of a parakeet by its color. The cere of a male is bluish, while that of a female is brownish.

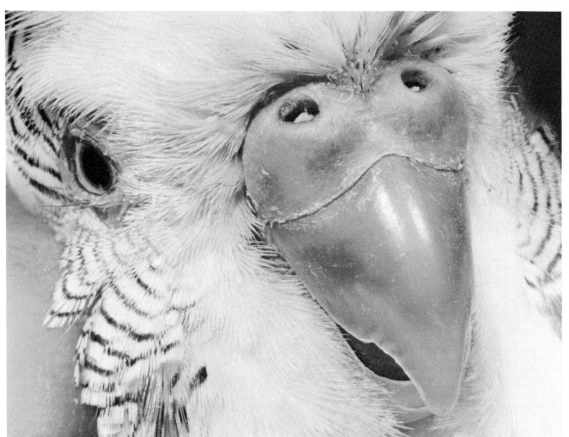

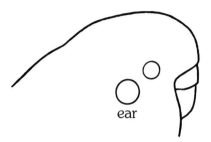

ear

Although you can't see their ears, birds hear well. Under the feathers on each side of the head is a round patch of skin. This patch is the bird's ear. Inside, a tube leads from it to the inner ear.

Birds of the parrot family need good hearing to communicate with each other. When flying, each bird in a flock of wild parakeets or cockatiels repeats a warbling call. And when the flock lands, the birds keep up a constant chatter as they eat. These sounds help keep the group together, since no bird will stray far from the noise of the flock.

41

Parrots and their relatives make popular pets because they are talking birds. Their sense of hearing helps them learn to imitate human words.

Talking birds may seem to have a special talent that other birds don't have at all. In fact, however, many birds can imitate sounds to some extent. For instance, most baby songbirds learn the songs of their species by hearing their parents sing. Scientists believe that talking birds simply have more of this ability to learn from listening.

43

The senses are important in birds' mating behavior. Cockatiels and parakeets use their senses of sight, hearing, and touch in their courtship.

Male cockatiels fan out their crest feathers, which the females respond to by sight. Parakeets will not mate readily unless they can hear the chatter of many parakeets around them. And both kinds of birds "kiss" with their touch-sensitive beaks during courtship. For this reason, these birds are sometimes known as lovebirds.

Parakeets and cockatiels do not build nests of twigs like many other birds. In the wild, they lay their eggs in the hollow limbs or stumps of trees.

Unlike most reptiles, birds care for their eggs after laying them. Each nesting pair protects the nest, and either the female alone, or both male and female, warm the eggs with their body heat.

After hatching, the young birds grow rapidly. At first, a baby parakeet is tiny and almost naked. But after only ten days it is covered with down.

At three weeks, the head and flight feathers have grown in, and the tail feathers are emerging from their sheaths.

47

Only one week later, at four weeks, the baby parakeet is ready to leave the nest. Its parents still feed it, but it has begun to try its wings, fluttering awkwardly from one perch to another. In a short time, at three months, the bird will be a fully grown adult, able to produce young of its own, and a master of the skill it was born for—flight.